Dazzling Digital Art

Cameron Macintosh

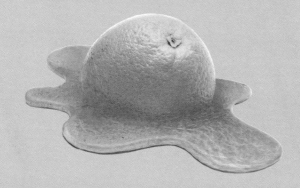

Dazzling Digital Art

Text: Cameron Macintosh
Publishers: Tania Mazzeo and Eliza Webb
Series consultant: Amanda Sutera
  Hands on Heads Consulting
Editor: Holly Proctor
Project editors: Annabel Smith and Jarrah Moore
Designer: Leigh Ashforth
Project designer: Danielle Maccarone
Permissions researcher: Catherine Kerstjens
Production controller: Renee Tome

Acknowledgements
We would like to thank the following for permission to reproduce
copyright material:

Front cover, p. 15: Shutterstock.com/Fit Ztudio; pp. 1, 11:
stock.adobe.com/portfolioa; pp. 3, 23: Shutterstock.com/PanicAttack;
p. 4: iStock.com/SolStock; p. 5: Shutterstock.com/rzulev; p. 6 (left):
Shutterstock.com/Inked Pixels, (right): Artwork by Ben Laposky, courtesy
Sanford Museum and Planetarium, Cherokee, IA, USA; p. 7: Courtesy of
the Computer History Museum; p. 8 (top): Getty Images/
Roger Ressmeyer/CORBIS, (bottom): Getty Images/Reza Estakhrian;
p. 9 (top): Getty Images/Langevin Jacques, (bottom): Alamy Stock
Photo/Agencja Fotograficzna Caro; p. 10 (left): stock.adobe.com/Nikolaos
Giannakopou, (right): iStock.com/Maxiphoto; p. 11 (bottom): NASA/
ESA/Hubble Heritage Team (STScI/AURA); p. 12: Shutterstock.com/
Pascal Huot; p. 13 (top), back cover (bottom): iStock.com/AlexandrBognat;
p. 13 (bottom): Shutterstock.com/MarbellaStudio; p. 14 (top): Getty
Images/Luc Castel, (bottom): Alamy Stock Photo/Malcolm Park; p. 16:
Shutterstock.com/Rawpixel.com; pp. 17 (top), 32: Shutterstock.com/
Master1305; p. 17 (bottom): Getty Images/We Are; p. 18 (top):
Shutterstock.com/Federico Magonio, (middle): Shutterstock.com/
Unknown man, (bottom left): Shutterstock.com/Corona Borealis Studio,
(bottom right): Alamy Stock Photo/CPA Media Pte Ltd; p. 19: Shutterstock.
com/J-Philippe Menard; p. 20 (top): Alamy Stock Photo/Mike Greenslade/
VWPics, (bottom): Alamy Stock Photo/ZUMA Press, Inc.; p. 21 (top): Getty
Images/SOPA Images, (bottom): Shutterstock.com/Lee Yiu Tung; p. 22
(top), back cover (top): 123RF.com/mbgraphicdesign; p. 22 (bottom):
Shutterstock.com/NSTIvectors; p. 23 (bottom): Alamy Stock Photo/veryan
dale; p. 24: Shutterstock.com/Shutterstock AI Generator; p. 25 (top):
Shutterstock.com/Shutterstock AI Generator, (bottom): Alamy Stock
Photo/Sergi Reboredo; p. 26 (top): Shutterstock.com/suriyachan, (main):
Shutterstock.com/Shutterstock AI, (inset): Getty Images/Fine Art; p. 27:
Shutterstock.com/Josep Suria; pp. 28–29: Jinhwa Jang; p. 30:
Shutterstock.com/Hero Images Inc.

Every effort has been made to trace and acknowledge copyright.
However, if any infringement has occurred, the publishers tender their
apologies and invite the copyright holders to contact them.

NovaStar
Reading age: 9–9.5

Text © 2024 Cengage Learning Australia Pty Limited

ISBN 978 0 17 033441 9

Cengage Learning Australia
Level 5, 80 Dorcas Street
Southbank VIC 3006 Australia
Phone: 1300 790 853
Email: aust.nelsonprimary@cengage.com

For learning solutions, visit cengage.com.au

Printed in China by 1010 Printing International Ltd
1 2 3 4 5 6 7 28 27 26 25 24

*Nelson acknowledges the Traditional Owners and Custodians
of the lands of all First Nations Peoples. We pay respect
to Elders past and present, and extend that respect to
all First Nations Peoples today.*

Contents

What Is Digital Art?   **4**

A History of Digital Art   **6**

Different Types of Digital Art   **10**

Digital Photography   **10**

Digital Painting   **13**

Digital Collage   **16**

Digital Art Installations   **19**

Pixel Art   **22**

Digital Art Using AI   **24**

Art for the Future   **27**

Rana's Review:
The Art of Jinhwa Jang (Response)   **28**

Glossary   **31**

Index   **32**

What Is Digital Art?

It's an exciting time to be an artist or a person who enjoys art. As new digital technologies are invented, artists can use them to create some dazzling artworks.

Digital art is any kind of art made with computers or other electronic devices, such as digital cameras, tablets or even phones. Digital artworks are also made by programs that use **artificial intelligence (AI)**.

With a tablet, people of any age can make digital art.

Digital artworks can be illustrations, paintings, animations, **multimedia installations** and even sculptures. They are often viewed on a screen, but some types of digital art can be printed on paper or **canvas**, like **traditional** artworks.

Digital art can not only look stunning – it often allows the viewer to **interact** with it or even to become a part of it!

People interact with the virtual waterfall of this multimedia installation by teamLab in Tokyo, Japan.

A History of Digital Art

One of the earliest types of digital art was created in the 1950s using the oscilloscope (say: *o-sill-o-scope*). The oscilloscope is a machine that was invented to study the flow of electricity. Although the oscilloscope is a scientific machine, artists discovered that the patterns on its screen could be used to make interesting images.

The oscilloscope was invented in the 1950s to study electricity.

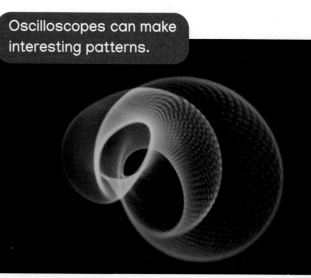

Oscilloscopes can make interesting patterns.

When large computers became available in the 1960s, artists began using them to make digital art. The earliest of these artworks were mostly lines in different shapes and patterns. They could be viewed on computer screens or photographed and viewed as printouts.

Artists were soon using these early computers to make all sorts of interesting artworks. For example, computers were able to draw simple line pictures using robotic arms, or make patterns of coloured lights.

This "drawing machine" was created in the 1960s using computer parts.

In the 1970s, digital artists found ways to make a wider range of shapes, including three-dimensional (3D) shapes. Special electronic tablets for drawing, known as graphic tablets, also became popular among artists. The artist would draw on the tablet with a **stylus**.

An artist creates a 3D shape on a screen using a stylus and a graphic tablet in the 1970s.

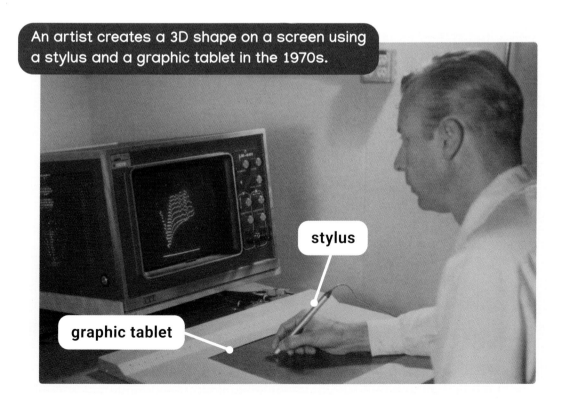

stylus

graphic tablet

A father and son use a computer to draw and print out a picture in 1983.

In the early 1980s, computer painting programs became available. These allowed people to paint digital pictures on their computer screens using the computer mouse as a drawing tool.

In the 1990s, computers became more and more powerful. People could save photos and videos onto them. Artists could use images from their cameras or video cameras to make art. They could cut and paste images from videos or photos to create **collages**.

This digital collage from the 1990s was created from images of the city of Los Angeles, USA.

At around this time, **software** became available that enabled artists to **edit** their digital photos or artworks. This software made it much easier for artists to change the look of a photo or artwork, or to adjust, or change, things they didn't like about it.

In the 1990s, artists and designers could use software to edit their images on a computer.

In the last few decades, digital art has become more and more interactive. The viewer is often able to become a part of other people's artworks. For example, they might walk through a multimedia installation and cause its lights and sounds to change as they pass by.

This interactive installation in Singapore changes as people walk across the floor.

Different Types of Digital Art

Digital Photography

One of the most popular types of digital art is digital photography. Until the late 1990s, most photos were taken using **film** cameras. These cameras captured images on rolls of film inside them. The film then had to be taken out of the camera and washed with chemicals. This was known as developing the film. Once it was developed, the film could be used to print the images on special paper.

A photographer develops film and prints photos in a room lit with special light that won't ruin the photos.

a roll of film

200 36 exp.

PROCESS C-41

35mm color print film

200

Using digital cameras, photographic artists can now instantly see their photos and easily make changes to them with software. They can use this software to create interesting **effects** in their photos.

A digital effect has been applied to this photo of an orange to make it look as though it's melting.

Cameras in Space!

This photo of a nebula, or huge cloud of gas and dust, was taken by a camera in space in 2012.

One reason digital photography was invented was to more quickly and easily see photos of space. Film cameras do work in space, but scientists used to have to wait for the camera to return to Earth to see the photos. With digital cameras, images can be sent back to Earth instantly.

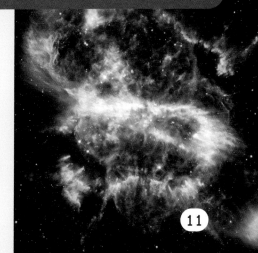

For many people, digital photography is a part of everyday life. People who have cameras in their phones can make their own digital art wherever they go. They can use apps to edit their photos – for example, to change the colours or brightness. They can even add to or delete parts of their photos to make unique artworks.

Apps on phones and tablets can be used to add funny effects to images.

Digital Painting

Digital painting is similar to traditional painting in many ways, but instead of using a brush, paint and canvas, the artist uses a tablet and a stylus. The artist can create effects that would be very difficult to achieve with paint and a brush.

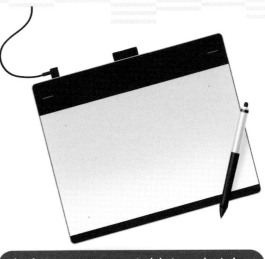

Artists can use a tablet and stylus to create amazing effects.

Digital artists can usually make artworks more quickly than traditional artists. It's easier for them to fix any mistakes, too!

An artist adds the finishing touches to their digital painting.

13

Many artists have discovered that they can create digital paintings using everyday devices, such as their phones. This can be a quick and fun way to make paintings that can be easily shared.

David Hockney

British artist David Hockney has painted many popular artworks using the software on his phone. These paintings often feature plants and colourful skies.

David Hockney

Some of David Hockney's smartphone artworks were displayed in an art museum in London in 2017.

With the invention of **virtual reality**, artists can even create 3D paintings that hover in the air. The artist puts on a headset and holds a digital brush. The lines they draw in the air seem to float around them while they are wearing the headset.

Digital brushes can be used to create virtual reality artworks that can only be seen while wearing a headset.

Digital Collage

A collage is an artwork made by combining different materials, or parts of other artworks, to make a new artwork. In a traditional collage, these materials can include photos, sections of paintings, clippings from newspapers or magazines, or even pieces of fabric. Now, collages can also be digital.

An artist creates a digital collage on her computer.

Artists can use software on their computers or devices to bring together different photos or other digital artworks. They can layer these over the top of one another or cut and paste them into place. Digital collages can even include snippets of video, such as animations.

Layering images in a digital collage can create interesting effects.

A digital collage can be made using many different photos.

Some artists use sections of old or famous artworks in their collages. By carefully arranging these pieces with other photos or videos, they can give them a new meaning.

David **by Michelangelo**

This digital collage uses the head of the artist Michelangelo's famous *David* sculpture.

This digital collage uses the outline of a famous painting by the artist Johannes Vermeer.

Girl with a Pearl Earring **by Johannes Vermeer**

Digital Art Installations

An installation is an artwork designed to fill a large space. An installation could be a collection of sculptures that people can walk among, or a large room that has been decorated in an interesting way.

A digital art installation uses digital technology to fill a space. It could be a large digital painting with moving images, or lights and images projected onto a building. Installations often include sounds or music, too.

Light was projected onto the Sydney Opera House to create this huge digital art installation.

Digital art installations are often designed to encourage audiences to interact with them. For example, the lights in an installation might change colour when someone walks under them.

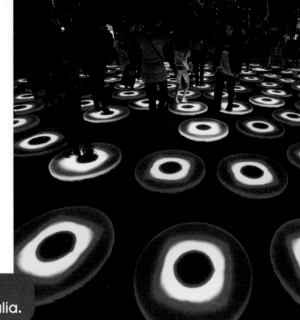

Tourists enjoy an interactive installation in Sydney, Australia.

Parents and children play inside a colourful installation at the digital art exhibition of the teamLab Future Park in Taipei, Taiwan.

Many popular installations focus on the works of a well-known artist. The audience can see the artist's paintings projected onto huge walls or on the floor. Visitors can have the experience of walking through the paintings.

Visitors enjoy a digital art installation featuring the famous artist Vincent van Gogh's paintings.

teamLab, Tokyo

One of the world's leading digital art studios, teamLab, is located in Tokyo, Japan. The artists at teamLab create spectacular digital installations that make the viewer feel as if they are a part of the art.

Visitors interact with a digital art installation at teamLab Planets, an art museum in Tokyo, Japan.

Pixel Art

Pixel art is a popular type of digital art. In pixel art, pictures or animations are made using pixels. A pixel is one of the small blocks of colour that make up a digital image. It takes many rows of pixels to make up a digital image.

Pixels are the building blocks used to make a larger image.

As technology has progressed, pixels have become smaller and smaller. However, most pixel artists prefer the **style** of art they can create using larger pixels.

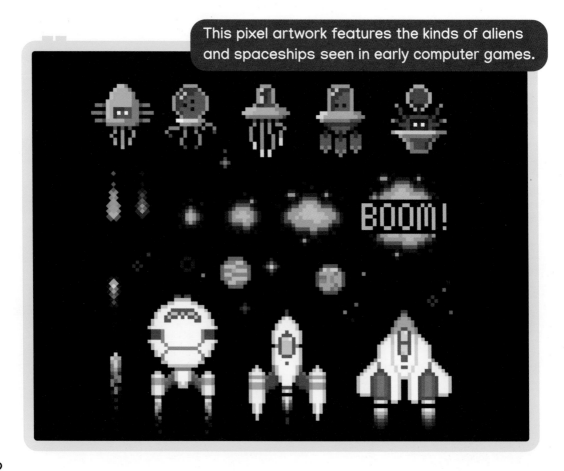

This pixel artwork features the kinds of aliens and spaceships seen in early computer games.

When an artist starts work on a piece of pixel art, they need to decide on the size and colours of the pixels they will use. Usually, the next step is to make a **grid** of squares, which the artist will fill in with individual pixels to make the artwork.

Pixel art is created by colouring small squares in a grid.

A well-known example of pixel art is the art style seen in the video game *Minecraft*. The characters and scenery in *Minecraft* are very simple and are based on large pixels that are easy to see.

The video game *Minecraft* uses pixel art.

Digital Art Using AI

Artificial intelligence (AI) is the ability of computers to perform tasks that people would usually do themselves. Computers can often complete these tasks much more quickly. One of the most exciting uses of AI is to create art. This type of digital art is known as AI-generated art.

AI-generated art is made by computer **programs**. The user tells the program what they want to see in a new artwork, and the program instantly makes it. For example, the user could ask for a cartoon of a lion driving a racing car. If the user doesn't like the artwork that the program produces, they can ask it to try again until it produces an artwork that looks just right.

A user can ask an AI program to try again if the first artwork isn't quite right.

AI art programs can even make new art in the style of real artists. For example, the person using the computer program could ask it for a painting of something from today in the style of a famous artist from the past.

This AI art of a rocket uses the style of artist Vincent van Gogh.

The programs then create the art by using information about existing art. They **analyse** thousands of artworks to find the most common features of their particular styles. The programs then use this information to make new artworks in similar styles.

The Starry Night is one of Vincent van Gogh's best-known paintings.

Many people have strong opinions about whether it's right or wrong that a computer program can instantly copy an artist's style. How would you feel if you were an artist and your style was copied by a program?

This AI art of a dog uses the style of the artist Claude Monet.

Claude Monet was famous for painting water lilies.

Art for the Future

As technology develops, digital artists will continue to find new ways to express themselves and create exciting new types of art. It will also become easier for all of us to share our artistic ideas with other people. Digital art will be a part of our lives for many years to come.

What technologies might the digital artists of the future use?

Rana's Review:
The Art of Jinhwa Jang

Today, as part of our homework task, our teacher Ms Perera showed us a digital painting by an artist called Jinhwa Jang. Jinhwa is from Taiwan. She now lives in Seoul, South Korea, and has won many awards for her artworks. I really like her art, for all sorts of reasons.

Jinhwa Jang

This artwork is called *Summer 3*, and it was painted in 2021. It shows two people with ice creams, walking along a stream on the edge of a city full of colourful buildings. A large white bird seems to be watching the people from the **foreground**. The faces of two women in rounded boxes sit on top of the picture of the city.

This artwork was made on a computer, using a program that allows the artist to draw and colour their artworks on screen.

I like the way Jinhwa has used lots of bright **fluorescent** colours as well as some more natural colours, such as blues and greens. This mix of colours makes me look carefully at the artwork and wonder which parts of it are meant to seem real and which are meant to look like a cartoon. The two people walking beside the stream look like cartoon characters, and the women in the boxes are painted in fun, unusual colours. The buildings in the background look realistic, even though they are brightly coloured, like the other parts of the artwork.

Summer 3 is a colourful digital painting by Taiwanese artist Jinhwa Jang.

I really like how the artist has included nature and the city environment in the one picture. I also find it interesting that she chose to include the women in the boxes. They seem to be looking at me and wondering how I feel about the other things in the artwork. They have stars and planets behind them – maybe they are visitors from another planet, telling us to remember that our Earth is a wonderful place?

I think this is a great piece of art, and Jinhwa Jang is a very interesting and skilled artist. It would look fantastic as a poster on my bedroom wall!

Glossary

analyse (*verb*)　　　to look closely at something in order to understand it

artificial intelligence (AI) (*noun*)　　the ability of computers to do tasks that are usually done by people, like writing text or making art

canvas (*noun*)　　　a strong type of cloth that artists often paint on

collages (*noun*)　　pieces of art made by combining a range of different materials, or by putting images together on a computer

edit (*verb*)　　　to make changes to a piece of work such as an image or a piece of writing

effects (*noun*)　　interesting changes to the way something looks

film (*noun*)　　　a strip of material used to capture images in a film camera

fluorescent (*adjective*)　　glowing with a very bright light

foreground (*noun*)　　the part of a picture that looks nearest to the viewer

grid (*noun*)　　　a set of lines that cross each other to make squares

interact (*verb*)　　to touch or make some other action and receive a response

multimedia installations (*noun*)　　large art displays that can include a range of media, such as videos, photos and sounds

programs (*noun*)　　sets of instructions that tell a computer what to do

software (*noun*)　　a computer program that has a particular purpose

stylus (*noun*)　　a pen-shaped tool used for drawing or writing on a tablet

traditional (*adjective*)　　done in a way that has existed for a long time

virtual reality (*noun*)　　a computer-generated environment that appears and feels real to the user

Index

AI art   24–26

artificial intelligence   4, 24, 31

collages   8, 16–18, 31

digital painting   13–14, 19, 28–29

film   10, 11, 31

Hockney, David   14

installations   5, 9, 19–21, 31

Jang, Jinhwa   28–30

Michelangelo   18

Minecraft   23

Monet, Claude   26

oscilloscope   6

photography   10–12

pixel art   22–23

tablets   4, 7, 12, 13, 31

teamLab   5, 20–21

van Gogh, Vincent   21, 25

Vermeer, Johannes   18

virtual reality   15, 21, 31